TRUMP

260 Presidential
Pearls of Wisdom

Sometimes by losing
a battle you find a
new way to win
the war.

You have to think anyway, so why not think big?

One of the key problems today is that politics is such a disgrace, good people don't go into government.

I have a great relationship with the Mexican people.

I actually don't
have a bad hairline.

We will make
America strong again.
We will make
America proud again.
We will make
America safe again.
And we will make
America great again.

Without passion you don't have energy, without energy you have nothing.

My whole life is about winning. I don't lose often. I almost never lose.

Private jets cost a lot of money.

The problems we face now - poverty and violence at home, war and destruction abroad - will last only as long as we continue relying on the politicians who created them in the first place.

It is time to remember that old wisdom our soldiers will never forget: that whether we are black or brown or white, we all bleed the same red blood of patriots, we all enjoy the same glorious freedoms, and we all salute the same great American flag.

I don't like losers.

We must speak our minds openly, debate our disagreements honestly, but always pursue solidarity.

I judge people based on their capability, honesty and merit.

Do you mind if I sit
back a little?
Because your breath
is very bad.

When somebody challenges you, fight back. Be brutal, be tough.

Well, real estate is always good, as far as I'm concerned.

I'm the Earnest Hemingway of 140 characters.

The day after I take the oath of office, Americans will finally wake up in a country where the laws of the United States are enforced. We are going to be considerate and compassionate to everyone. But my greatest compassion will be for our own struggling citizens.

I wouldn't mind a little bow. In Japan, they bow, I love it. Only thing I love about Japan.

Sometimes you need conflict in order to come up with a solution. Through weakness, oftentimes, you can't make the right sort of settlement, so I'm aggressive, but I also get things done, and in the end, everybody likes me.

Every time you walk down the street people are screaming 'You're fired!'

Owning a great golf course gives you great power.

What separates the
winners from the
losers is how a person
reacts to each new
twist of fate.

We need a great president.

Everything in life
is luck.

I'll drink water. Sometimes tomato juice, which I like. Sometimes orange juice, which I like. I'll drink different things. But the Coke or Pepsi boosts you up a little.

The point is that you can't be too greedy.

I have an attention
span that's as long as
it has to be.

If people can just pour into the country illegally, you don't have a country.

If I were liberal Democrat, people would say I'm the super genius of all time. The super genius of all time. If you're a conservative Republican, you've got to fight for your life. It's really an amazing thing.

I grew up in New York City, a town with different races, religions and peoples. It breeds tolerance.

My father was very
energetic. My mother
was very energetic.
He lived to a very old
age, and so did my
mother. I believe that
I just have it from my
father, from my
parents. They had
wonderful energy.

But I believe in fair trade, and I will tell you, I have many, many friend heading up corporations, and people that do just business in China, they say it's virtually impossible. It's very, very hard to come into China. And yet, we welcome them with open arms.

I've always said, 'if you need Viagra, you're probably with the wrong girl.'

It's always good to
be underestimated.

I support health care for people. I want people well taken care of. But I also want health care that we can afford as a country. I have people and friends closing down their businesses because of Obamacare.

I'm competitive,
and I love to create
challenges for myself.
Maybe that's not
always a good thing.
It can make life
complicated.

So Bush certainly wasn't the greatest, and Obama has not done the job. And he's created a lot of disincentive. He's created a lot of great dissatisfaction. Regulations and regulatory is going through the roof. It's almost impossible to get anything done in the country.

Money was never a big motivation for me, except as a way to keep score. The real excitement is playing the game.

Obama has no solutions. Obama has failed the country and its great citizens, and they don't like it when somebody such as myself speaks the truth about this. It hurts too much.

It's tangible, it's solid, it's beautiful. It's artistic, from my standpoint. I just love real estate.

Our military has to be strengthened. Our vets have to be taken care of. We have to end Obamacare, and we have to make our country great again. And I will do that.

One thing about television, it brings out personality. People are able to watch me in action. They hear my voice and see my eyes. Television brings out your flaws, your weakness, your strengths and your truths. The audience either likes you or it doesn't.

I have a Bible
near my bed.

Somebody made the statement that Donald Trump has built or owns the greatest collection of golf courses, ever, in the history of golf. And I believe that is 100 percent true.

The 1990's sure aren't
like the 1980's.

Jimmy Carter used to walk off the airplane carrying his own luggage. Do you remember that? I don't want my president carrying - I want the freaking Marines to be carrying his luggage, and they want to carry his luggage.

Experience taught me a few things. One is to listen to your gut, no matter how good something sounds on paper. The second is that you're generally better off sticking with what you know. And the third is that sometimes your best investments are the ones you don't make.

I feel a lot of people listen to what I have to say.

People assume I'm a boiler ready to explode, but I actually have very low blood pressure, which is shocking to people.

Part of being a winner is knowing when enough is enough. Sometimes you have to give up the fight and walk away, and move on to something that's more productive.

I've been dealing with politicians all my life. All my life. And I've always gotten them to do what I need them to do.

Well, yes, I've fired a lot of people. Generally I like other people to fire, because it's always a lousy task. But I have fired many people.

I think Ronald Reagan was one of the great presidents, period, not just recently. I thought he had the demeanor. I thought he had the bearing. I thought he had the thought process.

I'm the No.1 developer in New York. I'm the biggest in Atlantic City, and maybe we'll keep it that way.

It's not like I'm anti-
China. I just think it's
ridiculous that we
allow them to do what
they're doing to this
country, with the
manipulation of the
currency, and all of
the other things
that they do.

Hillary Clinton was the worst Secretary of State in the history of the country. The world came apart under her reign as Secretary of State.

If you look at what's going on with your gasoline prices. They're going to go to $5, $6, $7 and we don't have anybody in Washington that calls OPEC and says, 'Fellas, it's time. It's over. You're not going to do it anymore.'

The Veterans Administration is a scandal. It's corrupt, and what's going on is a disgrace. And, believe me, if I win, if I become president, that will end. The veterans will be treated properly.

If you're interested in 'balancing' work and pleasure, stop trying to balance them. Instead make your work more pleasurable.

Getting things done in this country, if you want to build something, if you want to start a company, it's getting to be virtually impossible with all of the bureaucracy and all of the approvals.

Mitt Romney has a great view on China and how they're trying to destroy our country by taking our jobs and making our product and manipulating their currency, so that it makes it almost impossible for our companies to compete.

If you get good
ratings, they'll cover
you even if you have
nothing to say.

You know the funny thing, I don't get along with rich people. I get along with the middle class and the poor people better than I get along with the rich people.

The Arab League tells us to go in and take out Qaddafi. We've spent billions of dollars already with respect to the Arab League. Billions of dollars, because they told us to do it. Why aren't they paying for it? They don't like Qaddafi. Qaddafi's been a terrible thorn in their side.

Anyone who thinks my story is anywhere near over is sadly mistaken.

I do have my ducks in line if I want to do it, but I'd love to see the Republicans pick somebody that was going to win and take over this country and frankly, to use the expression, 'Make America great again'.

I wasn't satisfied just to earn a good living. I was looking to make a statement.

I mean, there's no arguing. There is no anything. There is no beating around the bush. 'You're fired' is a very strong term.

I have had lobbyists, and I have had some very good ones. They could do anything.

I get called all these
horrible names by
Lindsey Graham, who
I don't even know.

The pact we have with Japan is interesting. Because if somebody attacks us, Japan does not have to help. If somebody attacks Japan, we have to help Japan.

People might not think that, but the Republicans have all of the cards. And this is the time to get rid of Obamacare. This is the time to make the great deal.

I have used the laws of this country just like the greatest people that you read about every day in business have used the laws of this country, the chapter laws, to do a great job for my company, for myself, for my employees, for my family, etcetera.

We have to straighten out our country; we have to make our country great again, and we need energy and enthusiasm.

I have women working in high positions. I was one of the first people to put women in charge of big construction jobs. And, you know, I've had a great relationship with women.

I understand the military. I know the military.

When I see the crumbling roads and bridges, or the dilapidated airports, or the factories moving overseas to Mexico, or to other countries, I know these problems can all be fixed, but not by Hillary Clinton - only by me.

Well, I am a Republican, and I would run as a Republican. And I have a lot of confidence in the Republican Party. I don't have a lot of confidence in the president. I think what's happening to this country is unbelievably bad.

We're no longer a respected country.

The whole world of debt has to be changed as far as this country is concerned. We have to create jobs and we have to create them rapidly because if we don't, things are just going to head in a direction that's going to be almost impossible to recover from.

If I don't get along with Democrats, I'm sort of, like, out of business.

I think Les Moonves is the most highly overrated person in television.

I could never have imagined that firing 67 people on national television would actually make me more popular, especially with the younger generation.

The Obama representatives like Robert Gibbs attack people viciously, but people like me will not be silent and will answer them back.

Windmills are going to be the death of Scotland and even England if they don't do something about them. They are ruining the countryside.

You have to blast to build in Manhattan. And the buildings went up in Manhattan because of the power of that bedrock. Once you dig that foundation - with dynamite - and once you secure that foundation, that building isn't going anywhere.

People are so shocked when they find out I am Protestant. I am Presbyterian. And I go to church, and I love God, and I love my church.

I love Wisconsin.
It's a great place.

I have made the tough
decisions, always
with an eye toward
the bottom line.
Perhaps it's time
America was run
like a business.

Forty Wall Street is
probably the most
beautiful tower
in New York.

I deal with foreign countries. I made a lot of money dealing against China. I've made a lot of money dealing against many other countries.

I've created tens of
thousands of jobs
over the years.

Every decision on trade, on taxes, on immigration, on foreign affairs, will be made to benefit American workers and American families.

We must protect our borders from the ravages of other countries making our products, stealing our companies, and destroying our jobs. Protection will lead to great prosperity and strength.

A lot of people don't like to win. They actually don't know how to win, and they don't like to win because down deep inside they don't want to win.

No dream is too big.
No challenge is too
great. Nothing we
want for our future is
beyond our reach.

It's a great thing when you can show that you've been successful and they you're made a lot of money and that you've employed a lot of people.

Hillary Clinton is not going to be able to create jobs, I will tell you right now.

I built a great company, one of the - some of the most iconic assets in the world, $10 billion of net worth, more than $10 billion of net worth, and frankly, I had a great time doing it.

Iran is not getting rid of any of its nuclear plants. They're not getting rid of anything.

Years ago, I predicted that Iran would take over Iraq. Iran and Iraq used to fight back and forth.

Many agree that the worst thing that could ever happen is if Russia and China get closer.

I have respect for Senator McCain. I used to like him a lot. I supported him. I raised a lot of money for his campaign against President Obama.

Remember, many
Republicans didn't
vote for Mitt Romney.
He didn't inspire
people.

You don't get a
standing ovation and
get boos, by the way.
They don't go hand
in hand.

We need strength,
we need energy, we
need quickness and
we need brain in this
country to turn
it around.

All of the women on The Apprentice flirted with me - consciously or unconsciously. That's to be expected.

I saw a report yesterday. There's so much oil, all over the world, they don't know where to dump it. And Saudi Arabia says, 'Oh, there's too much oil'. Did you see the report? They want to reduce oil production. Do you think they're our friends? They're not our friends.

In real life, if I were firing you, I'd tell you what a great job you did, how fantastic you are, and how you can do better someplace else. You want to let them down as lightly as possible. It's not a very pleasant thing. I don't like firing people.

In 2009, pre-Hillary, ISIS was not even on the map. Libya was stable. Egypt was peaceful. Iraq was seeing a really big, big reduction in violence. Iran was being choked by sanctions. Syria was somewhat under control.

I think I was born with the drive for success because I have a certain gene.

People love me. And you know what, I have been very successful. Everybody loves me.

I had great a relationship with the Hispanic - we had a lot of Hispanics in the school actually from different countries, Venezuela, from Brazil, and they all played soccer, and I was on the soccer team, and I developed great relationships with them.

So we really need jobs now. We have to take jobs away from other countries because other countries are taking our jobs.

There is practically not a country that does business with the United States that isn't making - let's call it a very big profit. I mean China is going to make $300 Billion on us at least this year.

'You're fired' was not a part of the deal. And when I went into the first board room, the very first one, I'm looking at these people, and I had to fire somebody, but we never thought in terms of the expression 'You're fired.'

I was a great student.
I was good at
everything.

To me, I love real estate because you can feel it.

I love Neil Young.
And he loves me!
We have a great
relationship.

I try to learn from the past, but I plan for the future by focusing exclusively on the present. That's where the fun is.

In the end, you're measured not by how much you undertake but by what you finally accomplish.

I think the big problem this country has is being politically correct. I've been challenged by so many people, and I don't frankly have time for total political correctness. And to be honest with you, this country doesn't have time either.

Thanks to Hillary Clinton, Iran is now the dominant Islamic power in the Middle East, and on the road to nuclear weapons.

Hillary Clinton's support for violent regime change in Syria has thrown the country into one of the bloodiest civil wars anyone has ever seen - while giving ISIS a launching pad for terrorism against the West.

We will be protected by the great men and women of our military and law enforcement and, most importantly, we are protected by God.

I've got the hottest brand in the world.

A little more
moderation would be
good. Of course, my
life hasn't exactly
been one of
moderation.

My big focus is China and OPEC and all of these countries that are just absolutely destroying the United States.

You know that ISIS wants to go in and take over the Vatican? You have heard that. You know, that's a dream of theirs, to go into Italy.

The Iranians and Persians are excellent at the art of negotiation.

I have the right temperament. I have the right leadership. I've built an incredible company. I went to a great school. I came out - I built an incredible company. I wrote the number one selling business book of all time: 'Trump: The Art of the Deal.

The Mexican government is much smarter, much sharper, much more cunning. They send the bad ones over because they don't want to take care of them. Why should they when the stupid leaders of the United States will do it for them?

I like the idea of amending the 1964 Civil Rights Act to include a ban of discrimination based on sexual orientation. It would be simple. It would be straightforward.

When I am president, I will work to ensure that all of our kids are treated equally. Every action I take, I will ask myself, 'Does this make life better for young Americans in Baltimore, Chicago, Detroit, Ferguson, who have as much of a right to live out their dreams as any other child in America?'

We share one heart, one home, and one glorious destiny.

When you open your heart to patriotism, there is no room for prejudice. The Bible tells us, 'How good and pleasant it is when God's people live together in unity.'

People are tired of seeing politicians as all talk and no action.

That's one of the nice things. I mean, part of the beauty of me is that I'm very rich. So if I need $600 million, I can put in $600 million myself. That's a huge advantage. I must tell you, that's a huge advantage over the other candidates.

I own buildings. I'm a
builder. I know how
to build. Nobody can
build like I can build.
Nobody. And the
builders in New York
will tell you that. I
build the best product.
And my name
helps a lot.

I think the World Trade Center should be rebuilt as the World Trade Center, only stronger and one story taller. I hate what they're doing with the World Trade Center site.

Obama and his attack dogs have nothing but hate and anger in their hearts and spew it whenever possible.

Somebody said I am the most popular person in Arizona because I am speaking the truth.

Politicians can't manage. All they can do is talk.

I want to lower taxes
for the middle class.

Obamacare is
costing the country
a fortune.

We will reinforce old alliances and form new ones - and unite the civilized world against radical Islamic terrorism, which we will eradicate completely from the face of the earth.

We have to go see Bill Gates and people that really understand what's happening. We have to talk to them, maybe in certain areas, closing that Internet up in some way. Somebody will say, 'Oh, freedom of speech.' These are foolish people.
We have a lot of foolish people.

Seth Meyers is highly overrated as a comedian.

I'm a bit of P.T. Barnum. I make stars out of everyone.

We will seek friendship and goodwill with the nations of the world - but we do so with the understanding that it is the right of all nations to put their own interests first.

Saudi Arabia makes a billion dollars a day, okay? They make a billion dollars a day.

Everything I do in life is framed through the view of a business man. That's my instinct. If I go into a pharmacy to buy shaving cream, then I'm going to look for the best deal on shaving cream.

I have a great, great company. I employ thousands of people. And I'm very proud of the job I did.

I was a Democrat for a period of time early on. And then I was also an independent. And then I became a Republican.

Everybody has their detractors. Some people say arrogance, of whatever they may say. I only have one thing in mind, and that's doing a great job for the country.

I do respect them; I have great respect for women. In fact, this is one of the reasons 'The Apprentice' was such a successful show for so many years, the audience of women was fantastic.

I'm gonna keep Social Security without change, except I'm going to get rid of the waste, fraud and abuse; same thing with Medicare.

We need intelligence
in this country.
We need a certain
toughness in this
country, or we're
going to end up like a
lot of the other places,
and we're not going
to have a country left.

You've seen my statements; I do very well. I don't mind paying some taxes. The middle class is getting clobbered in this country. You know the middle class built this country, not the hedge fund guys, but I know people in hedge funds that pay almost nothing, and it's ridiculous, okay?

We need a president
with tremendous
intelligence, smarts,
cunning, strength
and stamina.

We will follow
two simple rules:
Buy American
and hire American.

America will start
winning again,
winning like
never before.

In America, we
understand that a
nation is only living
as long as it
is striving.

We will build new roads, and highways and bridges and airports and tunnels and railways all across our wonderful nation.

I am very, very proud
to say that I am
pro-life.

I have very good
executives and great
children. They're
very good.

I always want to
think of myself
as an underdog.

I got a lot of credit for comb-overs. But it's not really a comb-over. It's sort of a little bit forward and back. I've combed it the same way for years. Same thing, every time.

We can't let people down when they can't get any medical care, when they're sick and don't have money to go to a doctor. You help them.

My father was a successful real estate developer, and he was a very tough man but a good man. My father would always praise me. He always thought I was the smartest person.

I've always felt comfortable in front of a camera. Either you're good at it or you're not good at it.

What I hate about Halle Berry is there's always drama around her. It's always fighting, automobile accidents, fistfights, boyfriends fighting ex-husbands for the child.

At the Super Bowl, when Beyonce was thrusting her hips forward in a very suggestive manner, of someone else had done that, it would've been a national scandal. I thought it was ridiculous.

What my father gave me more than anything else is great tutoring and a great brain. You know, my father's brother was top person at MIT, went to MIT, graduated from MIT, was a teacher at MIT, a professor at MIT, a great engineer. You know, I have very good genes.

There's always opposition when you do something big. I do many things that are controversial. When people see it, they love it.

If you love what you do, if you love going to the office, if you really like it - not just say it, but really like it - it keeps you young and energized. I really love what I do.

You learn their honesty, you learn their competitiveness. You learn a lot about a person. It's not that they have to sink the putt and there's a great deal of talent involved - but you do learn about how competitive a person is on the golf course, and frankly, how honest.

The way I run my business seems to be easier than the way I run my life.

One of the reasons that New York became great was that it's serviced by many, many different rivers and waterways. You have the Atlantic Ocean connected virtually right to it, and it's serviced by the East River and the Hudson River and lots of tributaries.

First and foremost, I'm a real estate person. And that's what I love the most.

If I am elected President, I will end the special interest monopoly in Washington, D.C.

Hillary Clinton has perfected the politics of personal profit and theft. She ran the State Department like her own personal hedge fund - doing favors for oppressive regimes, and many others, in exchange for cash.

Together we will lead our party back to the White House, and we will lead our country back to safety, prosperity and peace.

We will be a country of generosity and warmth. But we will also be a country of law and order.

The American People
will come first once
again. My plan will
begin with safety at
home - which means
safe neighborhoods,
secure borders, and
protection from
terrorism. There can
be no prosperity
without law and order.

Every day I wake up determined to deliver a better life for the people all across this nation that have been neglected, ignored and abandoned.

I have visited the laid-off factory workers and the communities crushed by our horrible and unfair trade deals. These are the forgotten men and women of our country.

I have embraced crying mothers who have lost their children because our politicians put their personal agendas before the national good. I have no patience for injustice, no tolerance for government incompetence, no sympathy for leaders who fail their citizens.

As your president, I will do everything in my power to protect our LGBTQ citizens from the violence and oppression of a hateful foreign ideology.

My opponent asks her supporters to recite a three-word loyalty pledge. I reads, 'I'm With Her.' I choose to recite a different pledge. My pledge reads, I'm With You - the American people.

Together, we will determine the course of America and the world for years to come. We will face challenges. We will confront hardships. But we will get the job done.

Americans want great schools for their children, safe neighborhoods for their families, and good jobs for themselves. These are just and reasonable demands of a righteous public.

From this day
forward, a new vision
will govern our land.
From this moment on,
it's going to be
America first.

Together we will make America strong again. We will make wealthy again. We will make America proud again. We will make America safe again. And yes, together, we will make America great again. Thank you. God bless you. And God bless America.

To all Americans, in every city near and far, small and large, from mountain to mountain, from ocean to ocean, hear these words: You will never be ignored again. Your voice, your hopes, and your dreams will define our American destiny.

We stand at the birth of a new millennium, ready to unlock the mysteries of space, to free the Earth from the miseries of disease, and to harness the energies, industries and technologies of tomorrow.

A new national pride will stir our souls, lift our sights, and heal our divisions.

I played golf with my friends, and then I started to play with the hustlers. And I learned a lot. I learned about golf; I learned about gambling. I learned about everything.

I win at golf. I'm a club champion many times at different clubs. I win at golf. I can sink the three-footer on the 18th hole when others can't.

I've met some great people that deal with me in the press. I've also met some people that were very dishonorable, frankly.

The interesting thing is that everyone in golf is just nice. You learn a lot about people playing golf: their integrity, how they play under pressure.

The U.S. has become a dumping ground for everybody else's problems.

Hillary Clinton may be the most corrupt person ever to seek the presidency.

I have great respect for the Pope. I like the Pope. I actually like him.

I describe Jeb Bush as a 'low-energy' individual, and unfortunately for him, that stuck. And it's true: he's a low-energy person. That doesn't make him a bad person.

I want trade deals, but they have to be great for the United States and our workers. We don't make great deals anymore, but we will once I become president.

If I was the governor of New Jersey, the George Washington Bridge would not have been shut.

We've had soldiers that were so badly hurt and killed. I want their families to get something.

I shake hands very gladly politically. I don't think you could be a politician if you didn't shake hands.

I've been making
deals all my life.

I'm a believer in the
polls, by the way.
Rarely do you see
a poll that's very
far off.

I rely on myself very much. I just think that you have an instinct and you go with it. Especially when it comes to deal-making and buying things.

I've become very successful over the years. I think I own among the greatest properties in the world.

The Hillary Clinton foreign policy has cost America thousands of lives and trillions of dollars - and unleashed ISIS across the world. No Secretary of State has been more wrong, more often, and in more places that Hillary Clinton.

I have visited the cities and towns across America and seen the devastation caused by the trade policies of Bill and Hillary Clinton. Hillary Clinton supported Bill Clinton's disastrous NAFTA, just like she supported China's entrance into the WTO.

President Obama almost doubled our national debt to more than $19 trillion. And yet, what do we have to show for it? Our roads and bridges are falling apart, our airports are in Third World condition, and forty-three million Americans are on food stamps.

I'm very strongly against tax increases.

I was a great student at a great school, Wharton School of Finance.

I give to everybody.
When they call,
I give. And do you
know what? When I
need something from
them two years later,
three years later,
I call them, they
are there for me.

Mexico's making a fortune off the United States.

The Pope, I hope,
can only be scared
by God.

I'm worth far too much money. I don't need anybody's money.

So many people are
on television that
don't know me, and
they're like experts
on me.

Ronald Reagan became not only a Republican but a pretty conservative Republican - not the most. But a pretty conservative Republican. And he's somebody that I actually knew and liked. And he liked me. And I worked with him and helped him.

I think that when you get right down to it, people do evolved on different issues. And, you know, I'm pro-life. And I was begrudgingly the other way.

I apologize
when I'm wrong.

I always look at it that
I work with my
employees as opposed
to them working
for me.

Sure, sure, I'd like to see Apples built in the United States, not built in China. I'd like to see them have factories in the United States. At least partially. They make nothing in the United States, virtually.

Speeches are much easier if you read them. I just find when I do that, it's harder to fire up the crowd.

I have made really some significant deals because I play golf.

Owning great landmarks such as the Empire State Building or Trump Tower or the General Motors Building or the Plaza Hotel - there are certain just spectacular landmarks - it's an honor; it's really an honor.

I will tell you this: I have a lot of fun with 'The Apprentice'. Now we have a book out. Books are prestigious. But there's sort of nothing like having the big hot show on television.

The golf facet of my life doesn't go with the rest of my life, which is a rough-and-tumble life. I work in real estate development, which is the toughest business, and I do it in the toughest city. I deal with ruthless people.

Americans will have a chance to vote for trade, immigration and foreign policies that put our citizens first. They will have the chance to reject today's rule by the global elite, and to embrace real change that delivers a government of, by and for the people.

The most basic duty
of government is to
defend the lives of
its own citizens.
Any government
that fails to do so
is a government
unworthy to lead.

Decades of record immigration have produced lower wages and higher unemployment for our citizens, especially for African-American and Latino workers. We are going to have an immigration system that works, but one that works for the American people.

It is time to show the
whole world that
America is back -
bigger and better
and stronger
than ever before.

I don't make deals for the money. I've got enough, much more than I'll ever need. I do it to do it.

I had tremendous success in show business - a star on the Hollywood Walk of Fame. 'The Apprentice' was one of the most successful shows.

It's my life. It just continues to go forward from 'The Apprentice'.

I think I will be a great president having to do with the military and also having to do with taking care of our vets.

What truly matters
is not which party
controls our
government, but
whether our
government is
controlled by
the people.

January 20th, 2017 will be remembered as the day the people became rulers of this nation again. The forgotten men and women of our country will be forgotten no longer. Everyone is listening to you now.

I will fight for you with every breath in my body - and I will never, ever let you down.

We do not seek to impose our way of life on anyone, but rather to let it shine as an example for everyone to follow.

Do not let anyone tell you it cannot be done. No challenge can match the heart and fight and spirit of America. We will not fail. Our country will thrive and prosper again.

We will bring back our jobs. We will bring back our borders. We will bring back our wealth. And we will bring back our dreams.

I've always won, and I'm going to continue to win. And that's the way it is.

We will no longer surrender this country or its people to the false song of globalism.

We will get our
people off of welfare
and back to work -
rebuilding our country
with American hands
and American labor.

When America is united, America is totally unstoppable.

And whether a child is born in the urban sprawl of Detroit or the windswept plains of Nebraska, they look up at the same night sky, they fill their heart with the same dreams, and they are infused with the breath of life by the same almighty Creator.

In July of 2004, I came out strongly against the war with Iraq because it was going to destabilize the Middle East.

I want to be a fair trader. I want to be a firm and fair trader.

Ever since 'The Apprentice' my life has gotten so much busier.

I've always been covered by a press that's mostly financial press.

I would say that
I bought the land
under which Trump
Tower sits while
playing golf.

You're fired.

www.ingramcontent.com/pod-product-compliance
Lightning Source LLC
Chambersburg PA
CBHW062132280526
45788CB00001B/146